Let's Take Care of Our New Dog

Núria Roca / Rosa M. Curto

BARRON'S

Welcome!

Today is a great day. Miranda, Mark, and their parents adopted Duke, a cute puppy that looks like a fluffy ball with legs.

This is Duke, and on the opposite page are the things he needs.

Don't forget to give him an I.D. tag with his name and telephone number on it, in case he gets lost!

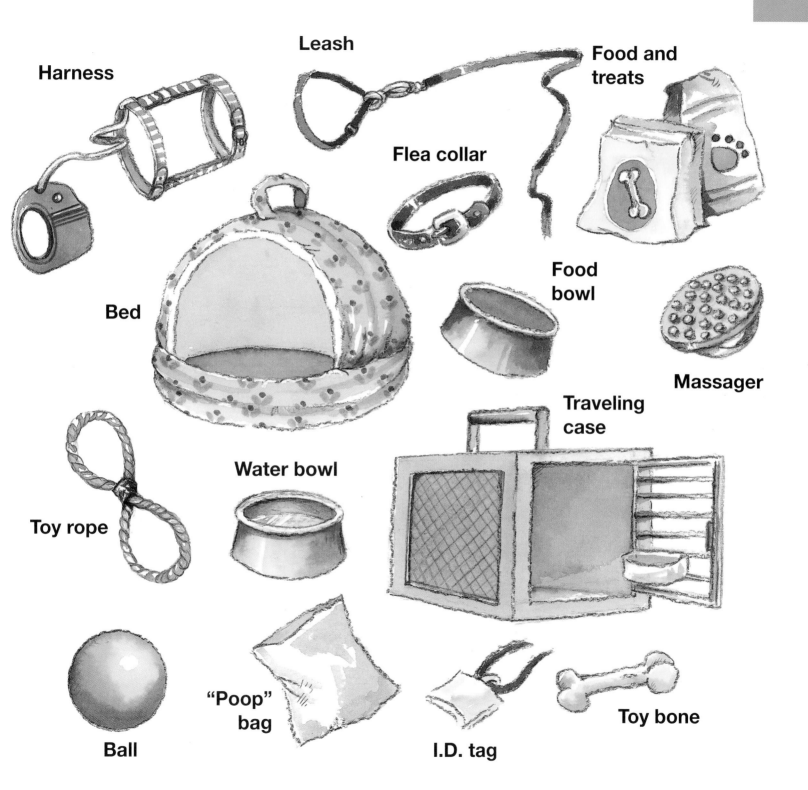

Harness

Leash

Food and treats

Flea collar

Bed

Food bowl

Massager

Traveling case

Water bowl

Toy rope

Ball

"Poop" bag

I.D. tag

Toy bone

Bringing the dog home

Having Duke at home is a big responsibility. The family will have to take care of him, teach him what he can and cannot do, play with him, take him out for walks, bring him to the veterinarian… Everybody at home will have to cooperate!

Miranda and Mark's parents made it very clear that the dog is not a toy, but another important member of the family!

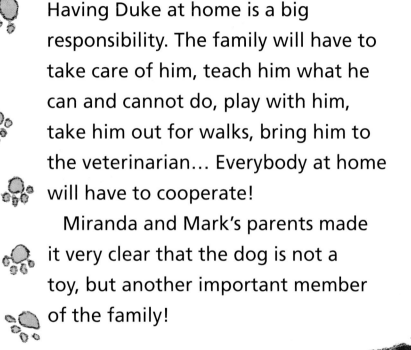

I love playing ball with my friend!

I like to go
for a walk
every day.

Time for my
medicine!

I never get tired
of being petted.

The doggy den

The first thing they do when they get home is let Duke sniff around and go into every room. He soon finds his special corner, with his bed and his food and water bowls.

Mark left a toy there, too, so Duke can chew it if he wants.

"This is Duke's den," Miranda tells Mark. "When he is here, you may not bother him in any way!" (Miranda is a little bossy.)

Holding
the dog

I can get hurt if
you lift me by
my front paws!

Never pick me up like this!

Ouch! My tail is
very sensitive.

One of the first things the children have to learn is how to pick up a puppy in their arms. They should not do it in just any way they like.

A puppy should not be picked up by his front legs.

A puppy should not be picked up by the back of his neck.

A puppy should definitely not be picked up by his tail!

To pick up a puppy, you should put one hand under his chest and the other under his rump. It looks easy, doesn't it?

"Doing his business"

The first lesson Duke has to learn is the place where he must "do his business."

This is the newspaper where the puppy must pee or drop his poo, but just for a few days. As soon as he is allowed to go outside, he will have to learn to do all that out there!

Miranda and Mark are eagerly waiting for their puppy to be vaccinated so they can take him for a walk!

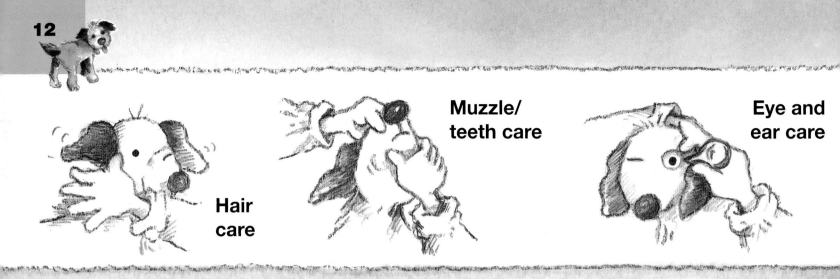

Hair care

Muzzle/ teeth care

Eye and ear care

Vaccinations

The first time they go to the veterinarian, Duke is a little nervous, especially when the doctor gives him a BIG shot. Fortunately, Mark pats him gently and talks to him in a soothing way. Now Duke has all his vaccinations, so he is ready to leave the house and go for a walk!

   "If a dog's nose is dry, and he does not want to play or does not want to eat, that means he is not feeling well," says Miranda. "I read it in a book Mom and Dad have."

Mouth care

Nail care

Out for a walk

When they put his leash on, Duke
seems to get mad. He bites it, he pulls
at it, and he scratches himself.

But then he notices the ball Mark tosses to him.
He likes playing so much that he forgets all about
the leash.

Mark and Miranda's mom always checks whether
the collar is too tight or too loose by putting
a finger between Duke's neck and the collar.
Mark can use two fingers!

A chewer

Duke still has his milk teeth (or baby teeth) and he spends the whole day chewing everything he finds—the sofa cushions, Mark's jeans, his dad's shoes…

The whole family will have to keep hiding objects from Duke until he is at least 10 months old.

When they catch him chewing something not meant for him, they firmly tell him "No!"

Little lessons

Duke already knows his name and what his family means when they say the word *NO*. It is now time to teach him a few more simple things such as "Sit!," "Stay!," and "Down!" But one at a time, of course, because otherwise he will get confused.

When he does something well, everybody congratulates him and pats his back and says, "Well done, Duke!" He loves it when everybody is happy and they play with him.

Now I am sitting.

I am thirsty!

When I'm resting, I feel good.

They told me to be quiet.

When I wag my tail, I am happy.

They feed me very well.

Good night!

I jump when I am happy.

I am a great soccer player.

Thanks!

Time to eat!

Duke is still a puppy, so he must eat more than once a day. Miranda and Mark take turns feeding him every other day. They have to put food in the food bowl at the same time every day and make sure that Duke always has fresh water to drink. And the bowls always have to be very clean! If they neglect their job, their parents have to remind them.

Now that Duke is full, it is the best time to take him out for a walk. This is a good opportunity for him to "do his business."

Doggy language

Miranda and Mark have learned a lot; when Duke carries his tail up in the air, it means he is pleased and when he wags it, it means he is happy!

When his tail is between his hind legs, it means he is sad, ashamed, or afraid.

But Duke also "speaks" with his ears and eyes. And with his barks— what a noise!

I love to play with other dogs!

Playing so hard made me thirsty, but my water bowl is empty!

I love to play "fetch."

My favorite time of all. . . meal time!

In the car

Duke is not used to riding in the car, so he is
restless and goes from one side to the other, barking
the whole time. When they stop the car, he jumps out and
immediately "does his business" right there. Yuck!
  Dog poo cannot be left just anywhere, so. . . it's time to pick it up!
  What Duke likes best about riding in the car is sticking his head out
of the window, but only when his family allows him to, of course!

A day in the country

Duke's family loves going out into the country to play ball, throw sticks, and swim in the river.

All of a sudden, Duke stands very still, staring at a point and pricking his ears. With his "super ears" he must have heard a sound nobody else can hear!

He also has a great sense of smell. "Playing hide and seek with him is no use," Mark thinks. "He can always smell me and ends up finding me!"

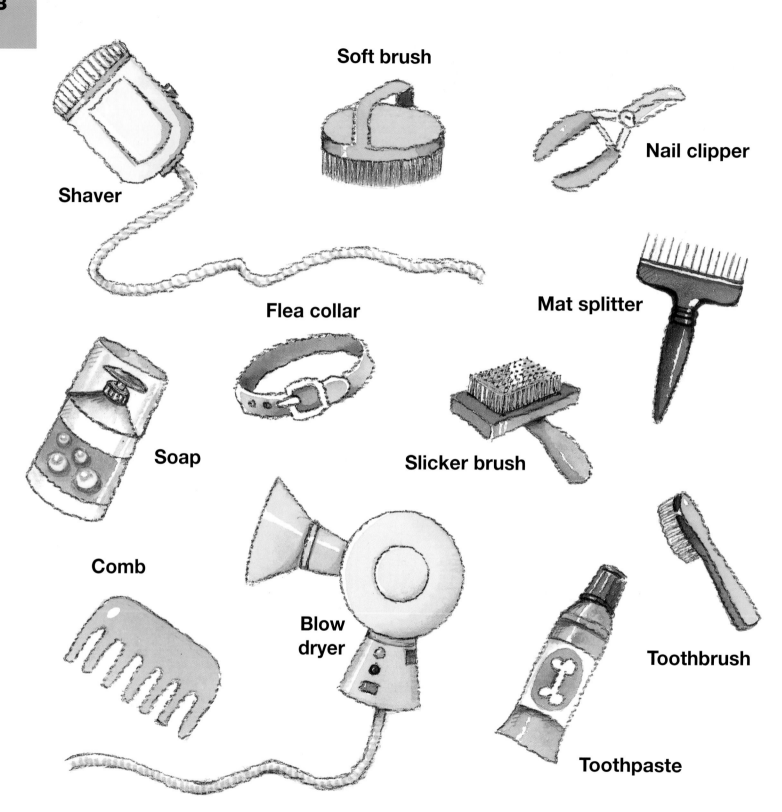

Shaver

Soft brush

Nail clipper

Flea collar

Mat splitter

Soap

Slicker brush

Comb

Blow dryer

Toothbrush

Toothpaste

Bath time!

Duke is very dirty, and he has mud all over him. When they get home, a good bath with lukewarm water is in order. When they are done, Duke shakes his fur and rolls on the ground.

"Watch out, he spatters!" warns Mark.

The items on the opposite page are just what Duke needs to look nice and clean.

Staying alone

Some dogs, when they are left alone at home, howl all the time. It is as if they are crying for the family to come home.

Duke, however, is used to staying alone for a few hours. Before they leave, mother or father take him out for a good run and Miranda and Mark feed him and play with him for a while.

They leave him a toy to keep him entertained while they are out.

That way, Duke does not get bored.

An incredible helper

Some dogs can pull sleds, look for people who are buried under rubble, or guide people who cannot see.

Mark has taught Duke to turn the light on and off and Miranda's best friend has taught him to pick up his pencil every time he drops it. When both friends are doing their homework together, Duke sits by their side waiting for the pencil to drop.

Duke loves having things to do!

We offer companionship to people with disabilities.

With our sense of smell, we help look for lost people.

We are the "eyes" for people who cannot see.

We love to bring the newspaper.

We provide good company for elderly people.

We never leave your bed when you are sick!

Activities

MAKING DOGGIE COOKIES
You will need:

– 2½ cups of barley
– ½ cup of sugar
– 2 egg yolks
– ¼ cup of margarine
– 2 egg whites
– 2 teaspoons dry yeast
– a little bit of salt (just the tip of a
  teaspoon)
– 1 ADULT TO HELP YOU!

1. Mix the margarine with the sugar until you get a smooth blend.
2. Add the egg yolks and stir again.
3. In a separate bowl, mix the barley, the dry yeast, and the salt together and then add to the previous blend.
4. Beat the egg whites until they stand in stiff peaks. Now, blend all the ingredients together.
5. Roll the dough into a thick roll. Use a rolling pin to extend it into a layer about as thick as a pencil.
6. Cut out the cookies using the shapes you like best.
7. Again, YOU NEED THE HELP OF AN ADULT TO BAKE THE COOKIES. Bake the cookies at about 425°F for about 30 minutes. Then, lower the temperature to 250°F and let the cookies bake until they are hard (leaving them inside the oven after it is turned off will turn the cookies very hard).
8. After the cookies are hard and cold, keep them in an airtight jar. Remember, you should not give your puppy too many cookies at once, only when you want to give him a treat as a prize and you have your parents' permission.

YOUR PUPPY'S FOOTPRINTS
Taking your puppy to school might be difficult, but how about taking his tracks instead? If you mix half a cup of wheat flour, half a cup of corn flour, and half a cup of water, you will be able to do it easily.

Mix both flours and then add water little by little until you get a dough that is soft but consistent, and put it in a dish. Wet one of your dog's paws and gently press it down to imprint his paw print in the dough. Wait until the dough dries (it may take up to a week). You may paint it in your favorite colors. When your puppy grows up, you can figure out how much his feet have grown!

Guidelines from the veterinarian

WHO'S THE BOSS?

Your dog needs to know who is boss at home to feel happy. But being boss does not mean mistreating others. A boss is someone who knows how things are done so everybody will feel happy; he or she must provide food and drink, take the others out for walks, teach what may or may not be done. . . being boss is a big responsibility! The puppy must know that at home, his bosses are first the parents and then the children. And if your puppy does things he should not do, just tell him "NO!" in a loud and clear voice and stop playing with him. You have to make it very clear to him that he may not bite or bare his teeth—not even if he is playing. And to be happy, your puppy needs a place of his own where nobody can bother him—not even you. This way he knows there is always a place he can go when he gets nervous or scared.

BEING WELL INFORMED

When you adopt a puppy, the first thing you need to do is go to the veterinarian, or animal doctor. He/She will tell you which vaccines the puppy needs and how many times you will have to take him to the veterinarian's office. If your puppy does things he shouldn't, like bark or howl when he is left alone, chew furniture, or prevent other dogs from getting close, the veterinarian will tell you where you may find a specialist in dog training. Also, he or she may recommend books you can read to become well informed!

THE FIRST NIGHTS AT HOME

If the puppy is going to sleep alone in a room, it's possible that he will whine all night. One way to prevent this is to put something in his bed that he used to have in his previous home, such as a little blanket or a toy. You may also place a clock near the puppy's bed, so the "tick-tock" may remind him of his mom's heartbeat. Your puppy may need a few nights to get used to it, but after a few days, he will get used to his new home and all of you will be able to sleep in peace.

GOOD FOOD FOR DOGS

It is very important to give your puppy good dog food. A pet shop is the best place to buy dog food. They know a lot about dogs and will be able to tell you what kind and how much food you should give your puppy.

It's very important to remember that foods people like may be very bad for your puppy. If you want to give him a treat, it is best to give special treats for dogs. These will not hurt him, and you may use them whenever you think your dog has done something well. Check with your parents first, though!

HOW TO WALK A DOG

When your puppy is about four months old, you should start taking him out for walks. He should get used to the sounds and smells of the outside world. The first few walks outside should not be very long.

Always take him on a leash. The first time he may not like it, but little by little he will grow used to it. And you must teach him to walk by your side and not to pull you, just as you do not have to pull him.

The best time to take a dog out for a walk is right after he has eaten—this way your dog will be able to "do his business." If he always eats at the same time and you take him out for a walk right afterward, your puppy will get used to a schedule. If your dog does poo in a public place, remember that you must pick it up and throw it in a garbage can. Dog poo should never be left out on the sidewalk!

OBEY

If your puppy comes to you every time you call him, tell him "good dog!" and show you are happy with him. Your puppy will soon learn to come to you when you call his name. NEVER use his name to scold him, because if you do, whenever he hears his name he will think you want to punish him and he will run and hide.

When your puppy is 3 or 4 months old, he may start obeying simple orders such as "sit," "stay," or "down." Just remember to pat him and congratulate him when he does what you ask.

SOME RULES FOR TAKING CARE OF YOUR PUPPY

- Be careful not to leave your puppy on his own near a swimming pool. If he fell in, he would not be able to get out.
- Young puppies should not go up or down any kind of stairs because they could hurt their backs.
- Never scold a pup for things he did some time ago. He would not understand why you are yelling at him. Scolding him is only useful when you catch him in the act of doing something he shouldn't.

LET'S TAKE CARE OF OUR NEW DOG

First edition for the United States, its territories
and dependencies, and Canada published in 2006
by Barron's Educational Series, Inc.

Text and illustrations © copyright 2006
by Gemser Publications, S.L.

All inquiries should be addressed to:
Barron's Educational Series, Inc.
250 Wireless Blvd.
Hauppauge, NY 11788
www.barronseduc.com

ISBN-10: 0-7641-3455-8
ISBN-13: 978-0-7641-3455-5

Library of Congress Catalog Card No. 2006921564

Printed in China
9 8 7 6 5 4 3 2 1